HOW IT HAPPENED

GUM

The Cool Stories and Facts
Behind Every Chew

GUM

The Cool Stories and Facts

Behind Every Chew

BY PAIGE TOWLER

ILLUSTRATED BY DAN SIPPLE

union
square
kids

NEW YORK

**union
square
kids**

NEW YORK

ISBN 978-1-4549-4498-0 (hardcover)
ISBN 978-1-4549-4513-0 (paperback)
ISBN 978-1-4549-4499-7 (e-book)

Library of Congress Control Number: 2022942714

For information about custom editions, special sales,
and premium purchases, please contact
specialsales@unionsquareandco.com.

Printed in Malaysia

Lot #:
2 4 6 8 10 9 7 5 3 1

12/22

unionsquareandco.com

Cover design by Whitney Manger and Liam Donnelly
Cover art by Becca Clason
Interior illustrations and series logo by Dan Sipple
Interior design by Nicole Lazarus
Created and produced by WonderLab Group, LLC
Photo research by Kelley Miller
Sensitivity review by Nina Tsang
Copyedited by Molly Reid
Indexed by Connie Binder
Proofread by Susan Hom
Image credits—see page 192

FOR MY DAD, WHO DIDN'T LIKE
GUM-CHEWING—EXCEPT WHEN I WAS
PLAYING SOFTBALL. —P.T.

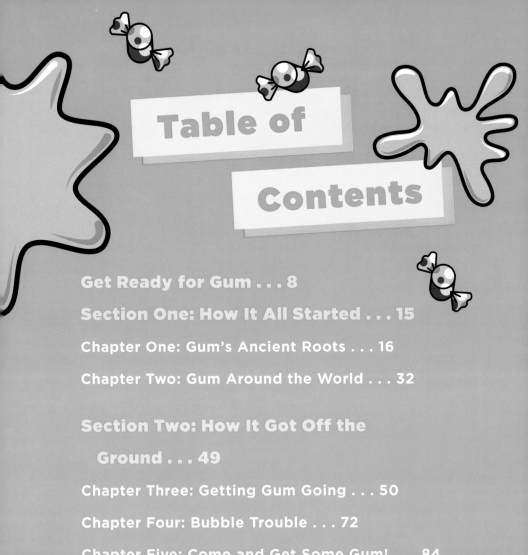

Table of Contents

Gum—It Seems So Modern, Doesn't It?

After all, the sticky stuff—from health-conscious sugarless gum to ballooning bubble gum to minty fresh sticks—is every-where. We've all watched people blowing bubbles in movies, bought packs at the store, and even stumbled upon chewed-up wads on the sidewalk. How different would our lives look without gum?

As it turns out, though, gum isn't modern. It's ancient.

The lives of Neolithic people six thousand years ago, living in what is present-day Denmark, looked very different from life today. Instead of going to school or scrolling on smartphones, Neolithic people spent all their time searching for food.

Since farming was difficult in the harsh northern climates, they gathered local vegetables and fruits and hunted ocean animals—much harder than grabbing a slice of pizza today! They also made their own homes and clothes out of animal bones and skin, built enormous tombs for their dead, defended themselves with flint axes, and . . . chewed gum?

That's right—some 5,700 years ago, someone living in this area chomped on an ancient version of gum and spat it out on the ground, where it remained for thousands of years until it was rediscovered by archaeologists.

But while that wad of old spit-covered gum remained unchanged for centuries, the culture of gum—and gum's influence on our lives—did not. Get ready to sink your teeth into the ins and outs of a tasty treat that has not only spanned the globe for thousands of years, but influenced history, art, television, radio, and more. It's time to find out how gum became the worldwide phenomenon it is today!

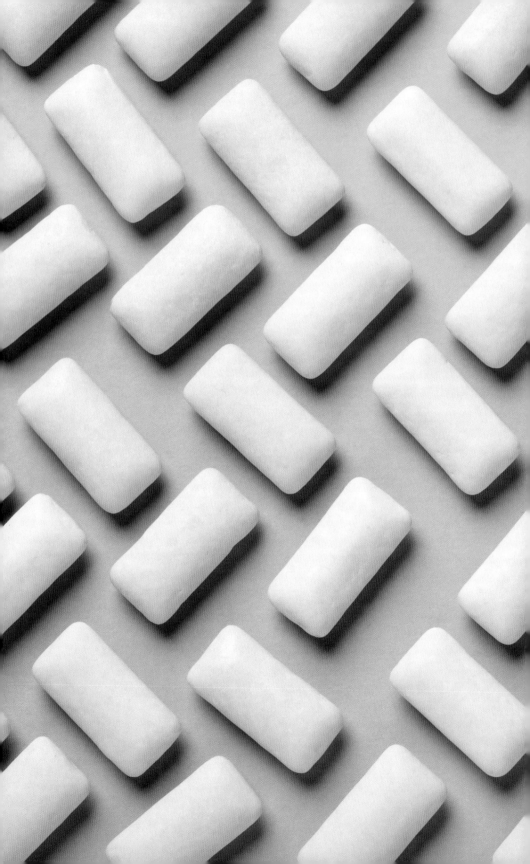

How It All Started

CHAPTER ONE

Gum's Ancient Roots

The Beginnings of Chewing Gum

If gum is so old, who came up with the idea to chew it? And what made them want to try it? Because when you really think about it, who'd want to put a sticky, rubberlike glob in their mouth and *chew*? As it turns out, a lot of people . . . for thousands of years!

We may never know the answer to *who* or *why* exactly, but we do know that people have been chomping on natural gums for much of human history—even *before* Neolithic Denmark.

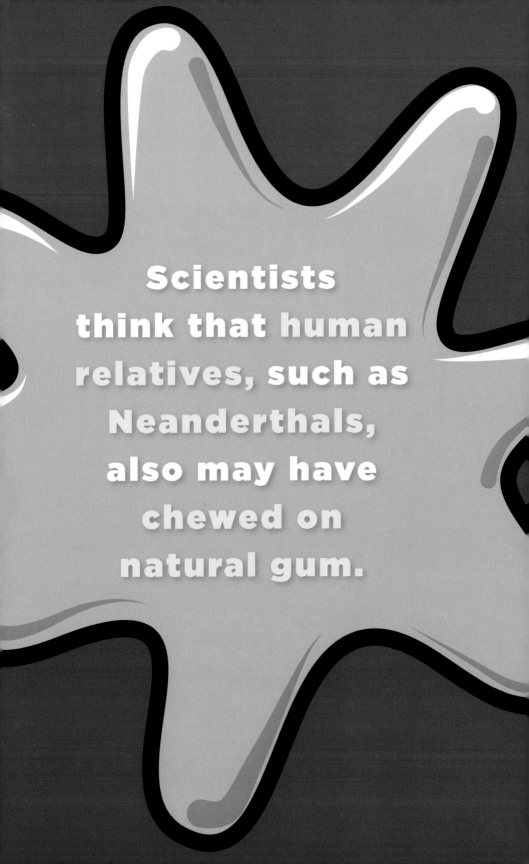

Scientists think that human relatives, such as Neanderthals, also may have chewed on natural gum.

Masticate

SQUISH!

In the early 1990s, scientists in western Sweden were hard at work excavating a Stone Age archaeological site known as Huseby Klev. The scientists had already found the bone remains of marine mammals that had been eaten by ancient humans when they came across something else: eight gummy black lumps, some of which were covered in tooth marks. These globs, called masticates (from the Latin word for "to chew"), were about the same texture as gum. They had clearly been chewed up and spit out . . . and they were more than ten thousand years old!

Who Was the First?

Will we ever know who the first person was to chew gum? Not likely . . . because the first gum-chewer may not have even been a person! Scientists have discovered that many primates chew—and even eat—natural gums like sap. Some primates known as gummivores—like certain lemurs and marmosets—survive almost *entirely* on gum! Gummivores spend much of their day searching trees for "gum sites" and eating the gum, which may give them certain nutrients they don't get elsewhere. Many even have special teeth that let them scrape away tree bark to get the sap flowing.

Marmoset

The scientists figured out that this early form of "gum" was made of birch bark tar, a substance made from the sap of birch trees. The Stone Age humans likely collected bark from birch trees and burned it. When the bark was cut away from the tree, the sap inside the tree would ooze out and harden, creating a protective bandage over the injury from where the bark was burned. Then the sap would harden into a sticky tar.

Stone Age people used this tar as a type of glue, likely to hold tools together or fix leaks. Chewing the birch tar probably made it more flexible and easier to use, so people may have chewed it before using it. But scientists also think these early humans may have chewed this "gum" for fun—not so different than we do today!

But did it taste good? Well, it wouldn't have been sweet like bubble gum. In fact, it may have tasted a bit earthy and smoky. If people chewed it for fun, though, it couldn't have tasted too bad!

Birch trees are found across much of North America, Europe, and Asia.

Gum-Chewing Ancestors

If you could create your own candy factory, would you have a room—or an island—dedicated just to gum? The ancient Greeks did!

Some of the oldest surviving written references to gum come from writers who lived more than 2,000 years ago. According to the Roman historian Pliny the Elder, ancient Greeks and Romans harvested natural gums called mastic. They collected mastic from bushes and trees in Egypt and Turkey, and they chewed it to freshen their breath and clean their teeth. But the most prized of all these natural saps came from a small island east of Greece, called Chios (pronounced HE-ose).

Where Does "Gum" Come From?

So if the ancient Greeks—and even scientists today—call gum "mastic" or "masticates," where on Earth does the word "gum" come from? As it turns out, "gum" likely comes from an even older word than "masticate" does. The word "gum" first began to appear in the late Middle Ages around 1300 CE as a version of the Old French word *gome*. *Gome* came from the Latin word *gummi*, which in turn came from the ancient Greek word *kommi*. But where did it all start? From the ancient Egyptian word *kemai*!

Chios, an island in the Mediterranean, has hot and dry weather most of the year, with cooler and wetter winters. Mastic trees—skinny-looking trees with twisting branches—grow on parts of the island. It's one of the only places on Earth where they grow. Ancient Greeks collected the hardened sap of these trees. After it hardens into firm white-yellow stones, the mastic tastes like pine and makes your breath smell sweet. The Greeks sold, traded, and chewed mastic as a natural chewing gum.

The ancient Greeks thought chewing mastic from Chios could also help cure stomachaches. Scientists today think that these gum pieces may have even helped keep teeth healthy by fighting off bad bacteria, too. Say goodbye to bad breath!

It's no wonder that this delicious and soothing gum quickly grew in popularity. In fact, during the Middle Ages, legends began to spring up about mastic. The gum came to be known as the tears of Chios because legend said the mastic trees began "weeping" sap after a Roman saint was killed on the island. Soon, so many people wanted the gum that it had to be carefully

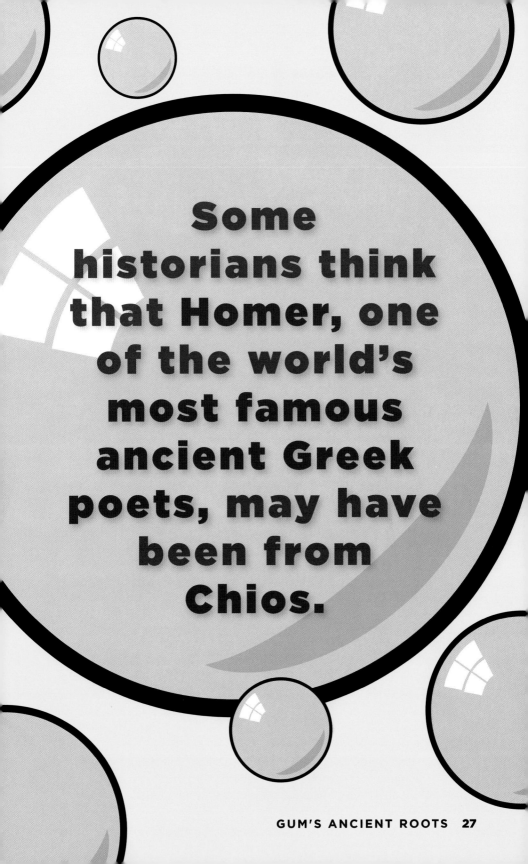

Some historians think that Homer, one of the world's most famous ancient Greek poets, may have been from Chios.

The island of Chios remains famous for its natural gum today.

guarded. After the southern Italian rulers known as the Genoese claimed the island in the twelfth century, they went so far as to build high walls and a watchtower—all to protect the chewy treat.

Even the fortress-like walls could not keep out the Ottomans, who established an empire spanning parts of Europe and the Middle East in the thirteenth century. Their empire continued to expand in the sixteenth century, and the island of Chios was among the additions. The Ottomans, too, treasured mastic, and even renamed the island "Gum Island." Mastic soon came to be a prized ingredient in many Turkish foods and desserts, including a type of sticky candy called lokum (also known as Turkish delight), ice cream, puddings, and even coffee. In fact, mastic was so valuable to the Ottoman Empire that the sultan ordered the execution of anyone caught stealing a lot of it!

Despite a bumpy history, Chios was able to stick it out. The island once again became part of Greece in 1913. And today, mastic is still sold and shipped around the world.

Lokum, also known as Turkish delight

CHAPTER TWO

Gum Around the World

From Atlantic to Pacific

While the ancient Greeks may have thought the mastic from Chios was the world's best, it was far from the only gum available. In fact, all around the ancient world, people were stuck on sticky, gooey, plant-based substances.

In parts of Africa—including the lands that today make up Mali, Sudan, and Senegal—people have been collecting gum arabic for centuries. This gum, made from the sap from acacia trees, is a light orange-pink with a rubbery texture. However, because gum arabic is somewhat tasteless, it is more often used as an ingredient or glue than as a chewing gum. Luckily for

Gum arabic is used in foods and drinks around the world today.

"One whose subdued
    eyes,
Albeit unused to the
    melting mood,
Drops tears as fast
    as the Arabian trees
Their medicinable gum."

—OTHELLO'S DYING WORDS
IN *OTHELLO* BY WILLIAM
SHAKESPEARE

A koala in a eucalyptus tree

many ancient Aboriginal and Torres Strait Islander peoples, the acacia trees in present-day Australia produced a much sweeter sap called *menna*. They also enjoyed chewing and eating the sap from eucalyptus trees, which are often called gum trees.

In addition to chewing the sap, ancient Aboriginal and Torres Strait Islander peoples also used the bark of the gum tree to make bowls, shields, and even weapons.

Mummy Gummy

Although it is edible—and even called *gum*—gum arabic was probably the natural sap least used for chewing. But that doesn't mean it didn't have its uses—in fact, gum arabic has been prized for thousands of years. So, what was it used for? Well, in ancient Egypt, the stuff was sometimes used to help preserve mummies! Thousands of years later, Renaissance artists in Italy found another use. Gum arabic was mixed in the paint they used to create their watercolor masterpieces. Today, gum arabic can be found in candy, drinks . . . and yes, chewing gum!

Some birds in Australia, such as the honeyeater and the pardalote, scratch gum trees and then eat the sap!

Other natural plants were popular to chew in ancient East and Southeast Asia. In China, Korea, and parts of Japan, people who wanted to freshen their breath or settle their stomachs chewed on ginseng root. If you've never tried ginseng before, you might find it surprisingly bitter. In East Asia, though, it has always been popular for its earthy sweetness and healing properties. Studies have shown that ginseng can help boost immune systems, lower blood sugar, and more.

In fact, ginseng was so important to ancient people in East Asia that there are even folktales and fairy tales about the plant. In one story, a young boy living in China some 1,500 years ago prays to a guardian spirit to help his sick mother. Later, he finds ginseng root growing on top of a mountain and feeds it to his mother. She becomes miraculously healthy again!

Meanwhile, Southeast Asia had one of the largest selections of natural gums in the world. Gum ghatti came from trees in India, Sri Lanka, Myanmar, and Nepal. Karaya gum, a sap taken from trees found across India and Pakistan, was used to help with digestion.

Salai gum was used both for chewing and for treating asthma in traditional Indian medicine. Gond, another type of gum made from the sap of acacia trees, was also used in Indian medicine.

Gum in the Americas

The Americas were also home to their own types of gum trees. In North America, many Indigenous peoples chewed on spruce gum, made from the sap of spruce trees growing in the Northeast. Some tribes also used the sap to treat wounds or sores and to help make canoes water-resistant.

For thousands of years, many Inuit peoples have eaten muktuk, the skin and blubber of whales. On top of being rich in protein and flavor, muktuk takes quite a while to chew, just like natural saps and other gummy plants.

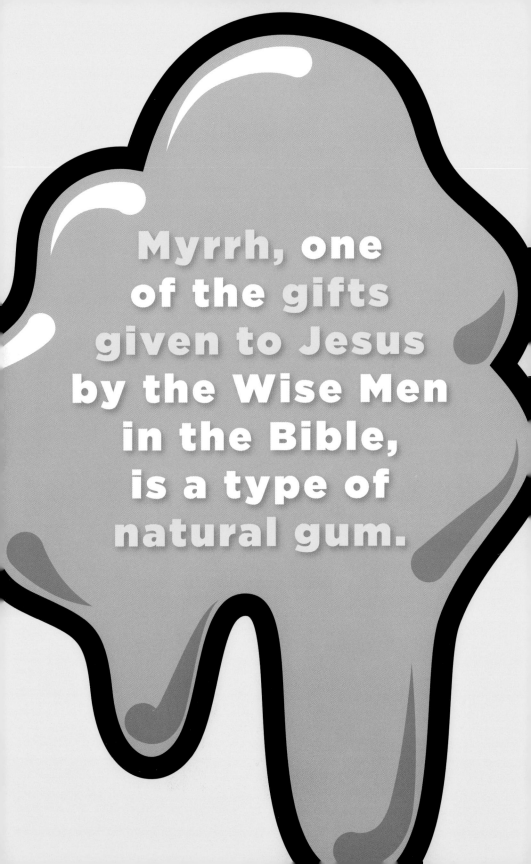

Myrrh, one of the gifts given to Jesus by the Wise Men in the Bible, is a type of natural gum.

Gum on Your Pancakes, Anyone?

Similar to how other Indigenous peoples of North America tapped spruce trees for their sap, the Anishinaabe people (pronounced ah-KNEE-she-NAH-bay) tapped maple trees for their rich, sweet nectar across what is now Canada and the United States. Today, many people are familiar with maple syrup in its liquid form, but for centuries, the Anishinaabe people have taken one extra step after boiling the sap down into syrup. They often cool the boiled syrup in snow, forming it into logs or cakes of hard, sticky sugar just like other natural gums!

"The (Aztec) men also chew chicle to cause their saliva to flow and to clean the teeth, but this very secretly—never in public."

—BERNARDINO DE SAHAGÚN, A SIXTEENTH-CENTURY SPANISH MISSIONARY TO THE AMERICAS

Sapodilla tree

In Central America, people collected the thick white sap of the sapodilla tree, known as chicle (pronounced CHEEK-leh). In ancient times, the Maya civilization existed across modern-day Guatemala, Belize, and parts of Mexico, Honduras, and El Salvador. The Maya peoples cooked, dried, and chewed the chicle, which they called *cha*.

The Aztec, whose ancient empire lay across modern-day central Mexico, also enjoyed chewing chicle, which kept their breath smelling fresh. Unlike other cultures of the time, though, they may have considered chewing gum in public to be bad manners. Imagine that the next time you pop a piece of gum into your mouth!

Many of the natural gums mentioned in this chapter are still used today. Gum arabic can be found in candies, paint, and shoe polish. Gond is used in inks, beauty products, and sodas. Next time you're at the store, look at different product labels and see if you can find anything that lists gum as an ingredient!

Gond

How It Got Off the Ground

CHAPTER THREE

Getting Gum Going

Sprucing Up Gum or Stealing It?

Considering that gum had been around for tens of thousands of years, it took quite a long time to truly catch on. But in the 1800s—known as the Industrial Age for the massive innovation and technological progress it produced—a man named John Curtis was ready to change that.

Born in Hampden, Maine, in 1827, twenty-one-year-old John Curtis had grown up seeing local Indigenous peoples enjoying spruce gum. Surely other people would be interested in the natural treat. Why not try selling it? However, as was all too common for the time, Curtis did not credit or partner with the Indigenous

John Curtis

community. Instead, he kept his plans to himself and began boiling the spruce sap atop his stove. He then cooled it in ice water, cut it into strips, and wrapped it in tissue. The final product? State of Maine Pure Spruce Gum.

At first, business was slow, with Curtis traveling from town to town selling the gum. But in just a few years, he had drummed up enough business—though none incorporated Indigenous peoples—to open a gum factory in the nearby city of Portland, Maine. Eventually, he had hired more than 200 workers and was cranking out 1,800 boxes of gum each day. Curtis even began to invent new flavors, like Licorice Lulu and Sugar Cream. Surely Spruce Gum was about to take over the nation . . . right?

Licorice root

Brilliant Inventions

Indigenous peoples of North America have always been innovators. In addition to spruce gum, they also invented hammocks, kayaks, and snow goggles. Next time you're paddling down a river or hitting the snow slopes, you'll have Indigenous peoples to thank!

Wrong. For some unknown reason, Curtis stopped making gum. This may have been because spruce gum tended to have a slightly bitter taste. Or it could have just been that Curtis got bored and moved on to other businesses. Either way, he became very rich, but the spruce gum industry fizzled out. It would take a long shot—something as wild as the chance meeting between an exiled president and an American entrepreneur— to reignite the gum industry.

An Unexpected Pairing

Antonio López de Santa Anna probably never expected to have anything to do with gum. As a young soldier, he helped lead Mexico to independence in its war against Spain. He went on to become the president of Mexico. In 1836, he was at the head of the victorious army that seized the Alamo during the Texas Revolution, when Texas sought independence from Mexico. Eventually, Santa Anna became a dictator—a ruler with total power.

By 1866, Santa Anna had been forced into exile from his home country and was living in Staten Island, New York. He wasn't quite ready to give up, though.

Why Gum Now?

The 1860s was a time of enormous change, conflict, and innovation for the United States. The Civil War, a war fought between the North and the South over the enslavement of Black people, began in 1861 and ended in 1865. Economically, many parts of the slave-holding South were left ruined after their defeat, but business was thriving in the North, where Adams and Santa Anna lived. Industrial innovations allowed some business-people—meaning white men at the time, as almost all women and people of color were forcibly excluded—to innovate and produce products much more quickly. Given how swiftly the country was changing, it was perhaps the perfect time for ambitious people to try to invent new products.

Upon meeting the American inventor Thomas Adams, Santa Anna came up with a plan he was sure would make him rich and allow him to return home.

Santa Anna had a habit of chewing chicle—the same natural gum chewed by the ancient Maya and Aztec. He introduced chicle to Adams with the hope of inventing a cheap alternative to rubber. For nearly ten years, Adams experimented with chicle, but could not get the results he wanted. Santa Anna, still penniless, eventually found another way to return to Mexico. But back in the United States, Adams decided to carry on with Santa Anna's concept—without Santa Anna.

Horatio Adams, one of Thomas Adams's sons, had an idea: Why not try selling the chicle as a chewing gum? He and his father added sweetener to the chicle, shaped and

cut it, and sold it to a local pharmacy. It sold out almost immediately. Delighted, the Adams family created Adams Sons and Company in 1876. The rise of gum had begun, though Santa Anna received none of the profits or the original credit!

By the end of the nineteenth century, more and more natural gum companies emerged as demand for the sticky stuff grew. Thomas Adams of Adams Sons and Company continued to sell his chicle product. For a while, he seemed to be the king of the gum industry, leading the way with many gum "firsts." In addition to his original unflavored chicle gum, called Snapping and Stretching, he created the country's first widely successful flavored gum in 1884 by adding shredded licorice to the chicle and calling it Black Jack.

Up until that point, gum had usually been sold in lumps. But Black Jack changed that, too. Using a machine he had created, Adams cut Black Jack into

the thin strips we know today, making it the first gum to be sold in sticks. And he didn't stop there. A few years later, he created the first gum vending machine. Located in a New York City subway station, it sold sticks of Adams's new gum called Tutti Frutti.

Tutti Frutti
ice cream

Old-School Ice Cream

The Tutti Frutti flavor first appeared as an ice-cream flavor in 1834. Meaning "all of the fruits" in Italian, the ice cream contained pieces of candied cherries, pineapple, and other fruits. The flavor was so popular that over the years, many different people claimed to have invented it. The flavor eventually fell out of favor when it came to ice cream, but it still lives on in Tutti Frutti gum.

More Gum, Less Soap

Back when Thomas Adams was launching Adams Sons and Company, fifteen-year-old William Wrigley Jr. was working as a humble salesperson with no idea that he would soon change the history of gum.

Born in 1861, Wrigley had started working as a traveling salesman for his father when he was just thirteen. He went door-to-door to sell soap. At the age of thirty, he moved to Chicago, where his father's company was selling soap and baking powder.

In order to gain more customers, salesperson Wrigley had the idea to give away natural chewing gum with every purchase of soap or baking powder. He worked with a local company, Zeno Manufacturing Company,

Mint has been used throughout history for its fresh flavor. Doctors in ancient Egypt even prescribed their patients mint in an attempt to cure flatulence.

to create gum from spruce tar and paraffin, a type of wax. Soon, he noticed something shocking: The customers were more interested in the gum than the soap and baking powder!

Wrigley changed his focus to give the customers what they wanted. He partnered with Zeno to sell two of the company's gum brands: Lotta and Vassar. In 1893, the enterprising salesperson took things further by creating his own gum brands. The first of these, Wrigley's Spearmint, sold a refreshing, chicle-based gum flavored to taste like garden mint. The second was Juicy Fruit, a sweet, candy-like chicle gum. It turns out that selling gum was a lot easier than selling soap—in fact, both Spearmint and Juicy Fruit still exist today.

At the same time as Adams and Wrigley were vying for the top spot in the gum industry, others were also entering the natural gum game. An inventor named Louis W. Mahle created miniature pieces of chicle gum shaped like squares. He called these Chiclets, and later sold them to Adams. By 1897, another rival gum factory located in Cleveland, Ohio, was the world's largest chewing gum factory. And in 1899, a pharmacist named Frank Canning invented a cinnamon-flavored gum called Dentyne. Not to be outdone, Wrigley himself debuted a third flavor of chicle gum in 1914, known as Doublemint. Amid all the competition and innovation, it seemed like nothing could stop natural gums from taking over the world.

65

Spearmint remains the most popular chewing gum flavor in America today.

Spearmint

Which Juicy Fruit?

It's juicy and it's fruity, but what exactly does Juicy Fruit taste like? While Wrigley seems to be keeping the exact recipe a secret, it's believed that the flavors include banana, lemon, orange, and pineapple. But curious fans have discovered another fruit with the gum's familiar taste: jackfruit. Found in parts of Asia, jackfruit is a large, spiky, green fruit that, when cracked open, contains a soft, yellow center. It is said to smell and taste like, well, Juicy Fruit. However, other flavor sleuths think the gum's unique taste comes from a chemical called isoamyl acetate, which can make candy taste like a mix of bananas and peas. Isoamyl acetate would have been widely available when Wrigley himself first invented the gum.

When Adams's gum first went on sale, it sold for a penny a piece.

"America is par excellence the land of the gum chewer."

—THE ATLANTA CONSTITUTION NEWSPAPER, 1901

Breaking Barriers

While Adams and Wrigley were making their fortunes, women and people of color were practically barred from the business industry. Did that stop everyone? Absolutely not. George Washington Carver was one of the most famous American inventors of the 1900s. He was born in the early 1860s and was enslaved until the Civil War, when slavery was abolished.

Carver grew up to become an agricultural professor, and he realized that the soil in the South was great for growing peanuts. At the time, though, no one was interested in peanuts or knew what to do with them. So, Carver researched different ways to use peanuts—everything from polish and oil to ink and glue. By the time he died in 1943, peanuts had gone from essentially nonexistent to one of the most profitable crops. Carver created demand so people could make a profit. Talk about a true business success story!

CHAPTER FOUR

Bubble Trouble

Gum in Demand

Thanks to salespeople like Wrigley and competition from people such as Adams and Mahle, by the 1920s, on average, each American chewed 105 sticks of gum every year. Chicle and other natural gums had become more popular than ever. In fact, they were a bit *too* popular.

As demand for gum grew, privately owned American gum companies bought out more and more supplies of chicle from Central American countries like Mexico and Guatemala. Chicle harvesters, or chicleros, had been collecting chicle from sapodilla

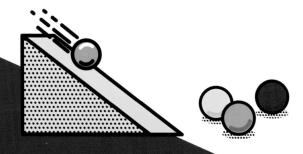

Sustainable Sap

Before Americans created demand for chicle, chicleros had been harvesting sap sustainably for hundreds of years, and still do today. These "gum-tappers" use big blades called machetes to slash the bark of a sapodilla tree, allowing its sap to drain. Sometimes they even harvest the sap high up in the tree, using ropes to climb sixty to eighty feet above the ground. After a tree is drained of its sap, the X-shaped slashes heal over. The chicleros then allow the tree to rest and regain its sap for as many as twelve years. The tree is not harmed by the process and can later be harvested again and again.

trees for centuries as part of Maya and Aztec cultures. Now the demand was too much: There weren't enough sapodilla trees, and there weren't enough chicleros. Companies abandoned the sustainable harvesting methods used in the past by the chicleros.

Instead, many of the sapodilla trees were being cut down completely! By the middle of the 1930s, one-fourth of the sapodilla trees in Mexico had been destroyed. Some foreign companies attempted to create sapodilla plantations, but they soon realized that the trees could not be farmed like other cultivated or planned crops.

On top of that, working conditions for the chicleros grew worse and worse. They worked long hours and were surrounded by dangerous animals like mosquitoes, snakes, and disease-spreading flies. Gum and chicle company owners grew richer while ignoring the risks they caused for their workers. In fact, some sap-harvesting companies in the early 1900s even brought in many foreign enslaved people and forced them to gather chicle.

It wasn't until the 1990s that locally owned chicle companies returned to a sustainable, safe method of harvesting.

In the meantime, many gum companies cruelly ignored the plight of the chicleros. But they could not ignore that their supply of chicle was getting chewed up . . . literally! In order to stay in business, the companies would need to find something just as sticky and chewy as chicle.

Gum, Unnaturally

So, what exactly is gum made out of? Chewing gum, natural or otherwise, consists of three parts: a gum base, a softener, and added taste.

For natural gums, the sticky base is usually a type of tree sap, like chicle. Sometimes the base is a wax, like paraffin. The rubbery, gluey base holds in the flavor and makes sure the gum doesn't dissolve in your mouth!

The softener helps keep the sticky gum base moist. It is usually made from vegetable oil or a moisturizing chemical called glycerin (pronounced GLISS-err-inn). The added taste usually comes from sugar and either artificial chemicals or natural flavoring, like Black Jack's licorice.

Why doesn't gum ever melt away in your mouth? Well, all things are made of small, natural building blocks called molecules. The molecules of gum bases naturally tend to stick together, meaning that they don't dissolve in water or spit! Your saliva can't break down the gum, but it can dissolve the sugar and flavoring in the gum until it loses its taste. Even if you had all the softeners and added taste in the world, you couldn't make gum without its gummy base.

Bubbling Up

Luckily, an alternative to chicle had already been in the works. Frank Fleer, an American candymaker, had been selling gum since the mid-1880s.

A Sticky Situation

Even if bubble gum isn't as sticky as Fleer's original recipe, it's still plenty gluey. Just ask anyone who's ever gotten gum stuck in their hair! This happens because the same molecules that help the gum base stick to itself also help it stick to anything else around. If you ever get gum stuck in your hair, water or spit won't help. Instead, oily products such as peanut butter or cooking oil will break down the gum base. If that doesn't work for you, you can also try using an ice cube to "freeze" the gum. Once it's chilled, the gum will lose its stickiness!

Compared to the success of his business rivals Adams and Wrigley, he hadn't had much luck. Fleer decided to set himself apart by creating something different: He would invent a gum that could be blown into a bubble!

For years, Fleer tried unsuccessfully to make bubble gum. He came close in 1906, when he invented what he called Blibber-Blubber. But the gum was never a success, as it was too sticky and fell apart quickly—and would even splatter when blown into a bubble. Gross!

Finally, in 1928, one of Fleer's employees found a way to improve upon the recipe. While experimenting with a rubber called latex, Walter Diemer realized he had accidentally stumbled on a flexible, less-sticky gum that was perfect for blowing bubbles. Unfortunately, he lost the recipe shortly after and had to spend months trying to recreate it. Once Diemer eventually "rediscovered" his discovery, Fleer began to sell the world's first real bubble gum: Dubble Bubble.

Bubble gum is pink because it was the only shade of food coloring available when Walter Diemer was creating Dubble Bubble.

Lesson learned: Always write down your brilliant ideas in a safe place.

Just like chicle, latex rubber had always existed naturally in plants. Around the time of Diemer's discovery, though, the technology for human-made rubber was booming. As chicle supplies dwindled, other chewing

gum companies turned to rubber as well. By the 1930s, almost all gum companies had switched to natural or human-made rubbers as their gum base, regardless of whether they were meant for blowing bubbles. Today, most gums are made with polyisobutylene (pronounced PAH-li-EYE-so-BEW-tih-leen), a type of fake rubber. That's right—chewing gum is sweetened, flavored rubber. Yum!

CHAPTER FIVE

Come and Get Some Gum!

The Art of Advertising

Given its humble and historical beginnings, how did gum become a craze that stormed the world? And how did it become an American icon in particular? The answer has to do with a combination of innovation, timing, and—most of all—selling power.

Over time, innovators like Adams, Wrigley, and Diemer had perfected chewing gum. But they still had to *sell* it. And that meant convincing customers to put a wad of sticky sap—and, later, rubber—in their mouths and chew!

Given how normal it is to chew gum today, it probably seems like an easy sell.

But gum could only become as common as it is today thanks to a little creativity and a *whole* lot of advertising.

William Wrigley Jr. led the advertising charge, applying his salesperson's expertise to his newfound product. He gave free display cases to stores so they could show off the gum to customers. Just like he offered free gum back in his soap-selling days, Wrigley also offered free bonus gifts with

gum purchases. And it worked! Just like their ancestors did, people found chewing gum to be fun and a great way to freshen their breath.

Then the Panic of 1907 hit the world. It was a financial crisis that caused many people and banks to lose money. But Wrigley saw an opportunity: The cost of advertising had dropped enormously. He bought tons of print ads in newspapers and magazines that touted the tastiness and the benefits of gum. Soon, Spearmint was the world's best-selling gum.

A Wrigley's gum ad, 1954

"Our four plants turn out enough gum every day to nearly bridge the Gulf of Mexico if the sticks were laid end to end."

—WILLIAM WRIGLEY JR., 1921

Wrigley didn't stop there. In fact, he cranked things up a notch. In 1915, Wrigley began an advertising campaign to send more than 8.5 million free gum samples to everyone listed in the American telephone book, a directory that listed people's phone numbers. He also tried to send two sticks of gum to every child on their birthday.

While he may not have reached every child, he succeeded at reaching more than 750,000 kids!

Wrigley also made ads that were aimed at adults, and at women in particular. In some ads, he claimed that gum could lower stress and cure upset stomachs. In others, he even claimed that chewing gum could make women "more beautiful" by helping them exercise their face muscles! At the time, it didn't matter if Wrigley's claims were true or not. By 1921, his company was making nearly ten billion sticks of gum each year.

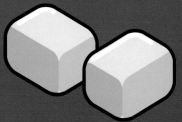

Ad Experts

Wrigley may have changed the gum advertising game, but he certainly wasn't the first salesperson to rely on ads. Some two thousand years ago in ancient Rome, politicians and shop owners painted ads on walls, just like modern billboards. And more than one thousand years ago in China, peddlers used rhyming songs to tell people about their wares. It wasn't until the 1400s in Europe, when Johannes Gutenberg invented an improved printing press, that printed ads became common.

A printing press with "moveable type" meant that people could quickly move letters around to create new sentences.

Bubblegum Bonanza

By the late 1920s, gum ads had become commonplace in the United States. Along with Wrigley, Thomas Adams also heavily advertised his gum brands, buying space in newspapers across the country. Walter Diemer taught Fleer salespeople how to blow bubblegum bubbles, so they could demonstrate to potential customers and teach them how to blow their own bubbles. This bubble-blowing strategy was worth the trouble. Soon, Fleer bubble gum was revolutionizing the gum industry!

"Gum chewing is another of those pleasures that is never proper."

—MISS MANNERS' GUIDE

A Horrible Habit?

While advertisements worked their sales magic, there were also many Americans who began to push back against gum. Like the Aztec before them, many people thought that chewing gum was a display of bad manners. Newspapers and manners experts ran columns on the subject, claiming that chewing gum was "loathsome" and "vulgar" and that it made a person's mouth look "unseemly." The manners columns especially—and unfairly—attacked women who chewed gum, calling the habit "unladylike."

By the late 1800s, New York and Chicago were the biggest **gum-chewing** cities in the world.

Many people even began to compare those who chewed gum to cows chewing cud— partially digested food that is brought back up into the cow's mouth. (That's why you should never kiss a cow on the mouth!) Newspapers encouraged people to chew gum only in private. As the popularity of chewing gum continued to grow from coast to coast, so, too, did the complaints against it, with some writers calling it an "infection." Culturally, gum was like any daring new fad: both intriguing and shocking.

Bad Ads

Salespeople knew that they would have to do something about gum's impolite reputation to keep sales up.

Some gum companies began to boast that chewing was a healthy habit. Dentyne, the gum created by a pharmacist, claimed that the gum was good for teeth and helped keep them "gleaming, sparkling white." Even doctors began to chime in. One doctor claimed that gum helped people pay attention and stay awake, while another said that gum could help people work longer and even run faster.

William Wrigley, on the other hand, doubled down on advertising to women. Did that mean that these new ads helped fight against sexist stereotypes? No. Instead, they enforced them by placing all the value on female beauty. The Wrigley Company developed gum-chewing "exercises" and said that women should chew gum twice a day for rosy cheeks. They also claimed that chewing gum would make a woman's eyes sparkle. By showing elegant women in evening gowns and jewels, Wrigley's ads also tried to make gum a fancy product.

Many gum ads over the next few decades would reflect horrible racist and sexist stereotypes of the time by using offensive images and slogans. In this way, gum was not only a part of the better parts of American culture but also the worst ones.

Scientists think chewing gum might boost your memory. Next time you're studying for a test, try it yourself!

"Hi-ho hey-hey! Chew your little troubles away. Hi-ho hey-hey! Chew Wrigley's Spearmint gum!"

—1960S WRIGLEY'S GUM RADIO AD

Jamming to Jingles

In the 1920s and 1930s, radios became more and more common in American households. In turn, gum companies altered their approaches to fit the new advertising format. Before radio, many printed ads had pictures and writing that told people why they should buy the product. But radio ads were shorter and could only rely on sound.

To make the most of this new format, gum companies began to use shorter, snappier slogans instead of long blocks of text. They also started creating catchy songs known as **jingles.** A jingle pairs a slogan describing a product with a tune that is meant to get stuck in your head, so it can help you remember the product being sold.

Have you ever had an ad get stuck in your head for hours? It was supposed to!

As television grew more popular in the 1950s, companies also set their jingles to videos in commercials. This made it easier to target certain audiences, from kids watching cartoons to parents watching the news. Gum had truly arrived.

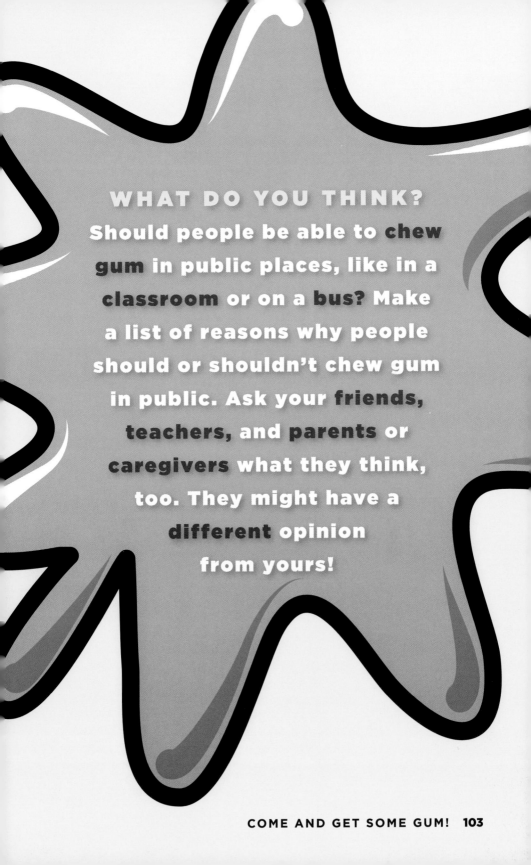

WHAT DO YOU THINK?

Should people be able to chew gum in public places, like in a classroom or on a bus? Make a list of reasons why people should or shouldn't chew gum in public. Ask your friends, teachers, and parents or caregivers what they think, too. They might have a different opinion from yours!

How It Took Over the World

CHAPTER SIX

A Stick of Gum for Everyone

Red, White, and Chew

In 1914, tensions in Europe, the Middle East, and parts of Asia caused one of the deadliest wars in modern history, today called World War I. The United States entered the conflict in 1917. The war became a part of America's culture—and with it, so did gum.

The soldiers who crossed the Atlantic to fight received pieces of gum as part of their rations, or their allotment of food. The military thought gum would bring them comfort, keep them calm, and help keep their teeth clean. Businesspeople, of course, began to run special ads that depicted soldiers with gum and encouraged families to send gum to those fighting.

WRIGLEY'S
SPEARMINT
SUGARFREE GUM

5 STICKS

"Wrigley's is the greatest wartime sweetmeat."

—WRIGLEY'S GUM AD

Suddenly, gum wasn't just a fun treat—it was a wartime necessity. Now, rather than seeing gum as rude and impolite, people began to see gum as heroic, patriotic, and even uniquely American.

POP!

A judge measures a contestant's bubble during a bubble-blowing contest.

Attitudes toward the "loathsome" cud began to change . . . at least, they did for men! Many people still carried double standards for women. Even after World War I, manners columns continued to claim that chewing gum was "unladylike." But lots of American women pushed back against this unfair idea.

Before 1920, American women were not allowed to vote. This meant that they had no say in their own government. Things were especially hard for women of color, who also faced racism and were often poorly treated by white women. But things very slowly started to change. In 1920, women finally gained the right to vote after decades of campaigning. Many also began to cut their hair short in "bobs," to wear

"If beautiful American women are to preserve their teeth . . . they will have to (do) more chewing."

—WRIGLEY CHEWING GUM AD, 1932

more daring clothing, and to take control of their independence. These women were often referred to as flappers. They were also known for chewing gum!

Were women finally treated equally in America? No. But gum had now become part of their culture, too. In 1939, a popular singer named Ella Fitzgerald cowrote and recorded a song called "Chew-Chew-Chew (Chew Your Bubble Gum)."

World War I ended in 1918, but soon, yet another global war erupted. In 1939, World War II began when Adolf Hitler, a German dictator, invaded Poland. Once more, American soldiers went to war. Gum was again included in their meals, and gum ads had patriotic themes.

World War II changed gum itself. Because of shortages in sugar, rubber, and chicle, many gum companies took their products off the market to focus only on making gum for the troops. When the Wrigley Company dedicated all its traditional gums to troops fighting overseas, it created something

new for customers at home: a replacement gum called Orbit. Made with lower-quality ingredients and no sugar, Orbit was meant to be a simple replacement that could hold people over until the war ended. Little did the company know that Orbit would still be popular today!

Bazooka Bubble Gum came out shortly after World War II ended in 1945. It came in red, white, and blue packaging to match the patriotic times.

American Gum Abroad

As American soldiers went abroad, so did gum. People all over the world had, of course, been chewing on natural saps for thousands of years, but now they began to see the appeal in the factory-made stuff, too.

In 1941, a young Korean entrepreneur named Shin Kyuk-ho left Korea to try and make a life in Japan. There, during World War II, he spotted American soldiers handing out pieces of gum to local children. Shin had the idea to open his own local gum business, and he founded the Lotte gum manufacturing company in 1948. Lotte's flavors, including Orange Gum and Cowboy Gum, quickly became very popular in Japan and South Korea.

Meanwhile just outside Milan, Italy, two brothers were also becoming interested in candies. In 1946, Ambrogio and Egidio Perfetti started running the candy company that would come to be called Perfetti. A few years later, they began offering their own gum. Inspired by American gum culture, Perfetti's gum was called Brooklyn, after the borough in New York City.

A pack of Lotte gum

A coffee company once released a blended coffee drink meant to taste like bubble gum.

In 1937, Don Go Peng Kuan founded a candy company in the Philippines named Columbia. The company introduced its own gum that was designed to appeal to Filipinos, with flavors that included mint cherry and tropical fruits. Columbia's gum also coated your tongue in different colors!

In countries where natural gums already had a long history, more and more companies opened to satisfy growing demand. In 1925, Canel's was founded in Mexico to sell chicle-based gums. Guar gum, a natural gum made from beans found in India, became incredibly popular in the 1940s and 1950s for its use in cooking.

Gum also changed to reflect local cultural tastes. Korean brand Lotte began offering ginseng-flavored gum, alluding back to when their ancestors chewed ginseng root. One of the most popular gums in Mexico

A large piece of gum is rolled out in Japan. Created in 2013 by Lotte, it was the largest chewing-gum stick at the time!

today tastes like tamarind, a popular sweet-and-sour flavor.

For thousands of years, gum had been a worldwide phenomenon, only to become a uniquely American product and cultural habit in the early 1900s. But once again, people all around the world couldn't get enough of the satisfying chew!

Gimme Gum!

More gum flavors, candy, and packaging appeared—especially for kids. Companies around the world came out with exciting flavors like sour apple, watermelon, pineapple, and more. They also released neon green gum, rainbow gum, and even produced gumballs made to look like baseballs.

Some companies became more creative with their offerings. Fleer Corporation created Dubble Bubble Fizzers gumballs, which fizzed like soda when people put them in their mouths. The first gum with a liquid center appeared in Mexico and Brazil in the 1980s. Charms Candy Company offered a lollipop that had gum hidden inside—and a clever ad to go with it, in which kids try to guess how many licks it will take to get to the gum.

Other companies changed their packaging to look sillier and more fun. American kids in the late 1980s adored Hubba Bubba Bubble Tape, which included six feet of gum in a package that looked like a tape measure. Another company sold powdered gum in packages that looked like laundry detergent containers! And soon people could even buy gum with their favorite cartoon, anime, movie, and book characters on it.

Flavor of the Month

Lots of gum flavors—from cinnamon to fruity flavors to mint—seem like obvious slam dunks. Others? Not so much! Whether they are meant for shock value or for more adventurous eaters, here are some of the stranger flavors of gum on the market:

- Italian Meatball
- Bacon
- Pickle
- Thanksgiving Dinner
- Popcorn and Soda
- Cat Hairball (Okay, this one just looks like cat hairballs . . . it tastes like bubble gum!)
- Ghost Pepper

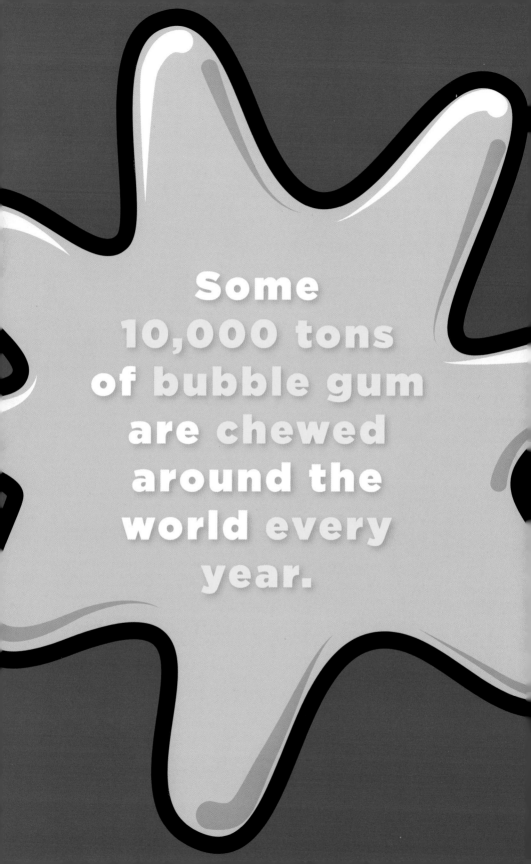

Some 10,000 tons of bubble gum are chewed around the world every year.

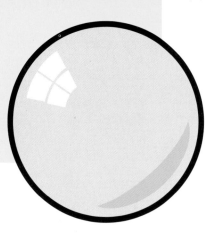

CHAPTER SEVEN

Gum and Games

A Home Run for Gum

Cal Ripken Jr., Luis Gonzalez, Derek Jeter, Shohei Ohtani—what do these four people have in common? They are famous professional baseball players . . . and they all love chewing gum during games!

Baseball and gum became intertwined early on, albeit behind the scenes. In 1916, the king of gum himself, William Wrigley Jr., became one of the owners of the Cubs, a Chicago professional baseball team. Five years later, he became the sole owner. In 1926, he renamed their home field Wrigley

Baseball and gum
have become intertwined
over the decades.

Field (which it is still called today). Much of Wrigley's gum fortune was poured into the team and the stadium, and many Wrigley's gum ads featured baseball players. Chewing wads to stay focused, players across the nation took part in the gum craze. Fans in the stands also purchased gum and chewed it while they watched.

Women's baseball also has a surprising connection to gum. Believe it or not, Philip Wrigley, son of William Wrigley Jr., had a hand in bringing women's sports to the big leagues. During World War II, male baseball players across the nation had joined the war as soldiers, leaving stadiums empty. Philip Wrigley, worried that teams

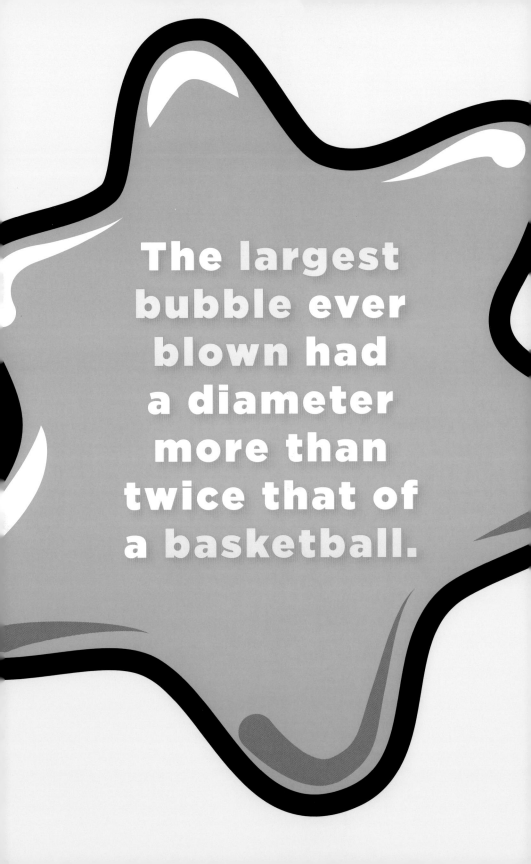

The largest
bubble ever
blown had
a diameter
more than
twice that of
a basketball.

Blowing Away the Competition

On August 8, 2014, hundreds of twelve-year-olds from all around the world arrived in Maryland to play in the Cal Ripken World Series. They were also going to try to beat a world record: most people blowing a bubblegum bubble at the same time! To beat the record, participants would have to follow two rules: They would need to chew their gum for one whole minute, and then blow a bubble and hold it—without bursting—for another thirty seconds.

That day, 721 baseball players, coaches, and fans set a new world record. Then, four years later, athletes and fans at a Minor League baseball game stepped up to the challenge. New York Yankees legend Bernie Williams led 881 people as they blew bubbles simultaneously!

would disband and that stadiums would go bankrupt, sought a solution. In 1943, with the aid of several businesspeople, he formed a baseball league with female players: the All-American Girls Professional Baseball League (AAGPBL). Although women had been playing softball for nearly half a century, they were rarely taken seriously as competitors and athletes at the time. But the women of the AAGPBL stunned spectators—and opened minds—with their fierce skills and spirit. The professional baseball and softball players made enormous strides for women in sports . . . with help from Wrigley's gum empire!

Make a Trade!

Baseball and gum also stuck together when it came to cards—baseball cards, that is. In the early 1900s, baseball cards were included as bonuses alongside tobacco products like cigarettes or chewing tobacco. It soon became clear, however, that the adults buying these products were not all that interested in the baseball cards. So instead, in the 1930s the makers of baseball cards turned to businesses like the Fleer Corporation to include baseball cards alongside candy.

In 1938, Morris Shorin's children created Topps Chewing Gum Incorporated. In 1951, Topps began pairing their candy with baseball cards, too. At first, they sold the cards with gum's chewy, sticky rival: taffy.

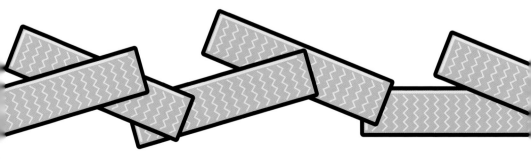

Some baseball players keep track of how many outs have been made in an inning by chewing a new stick of gum for each out.

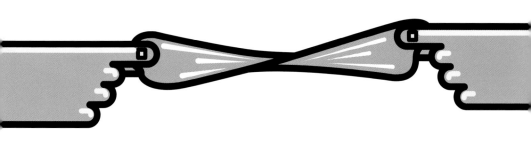

But the card's shiny coating had a habit of transferring onto the taffy itself, resulting in a unpleasant flavor that was tough to swallow. So, in 1952, Topps began selling the baseball cards with another treat that customers naturally didn't need to swallow: gum!

While kids were collecting baseball cards, people were slowly starting to learn about the dangers of tobacco. Many baseball players, who had previous gnawed on chewing tobacco to focus during games, switched to sweet, sugary chewing gum.

In the 1970s and 1980s, anti-tobacco health campaigns began to encourage people to stay away from the poisonous stuff. One baseball player in particular, Robert Nelson, was searching for an alternative to chewing tobacco. He came up with the idea of selling shredded pieces of chewing gum in a pouch, and Big League Chew was born in 1977. The gum appealed to kids, adults, and—most of all—baseball players, forever sealing the pastimes of chewing gum and baseball together. Today, Big League Chew has sold more than 500 million pouches of gum to date.

In Japan, one of Lotte's most popular early flavors was called Baseball Gum.

Gumballin'

Baseball isn't the only sport where players chew gum. Basketball teams always have a stash of chewing gum stored in their locker rooms. Michael Jordan, one of the most famous basketball players of all time, often chewed gum during games. One of his favorites was watermelon-flavored Bubblicious.

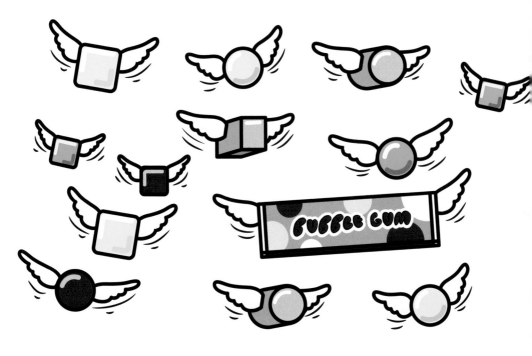

In 1998, Jordan, a member of the Chicago Bulls, played in the NBA finals. Before Game 2 of the finals, however, someone discovered that the locker room had run out of gum! One of the team's assistants had to run to a nearby gas station to find more packs of watermelon gum before the game. The Bulls went on to win the game and the championship title, too. Who knows— maybe watermelon gum was just the piece of luck that Jordan needed to play his best!

> **"Flattery is like chewing gum. Enjoy it but don't swallow it."**
>
> —HANK KETCHAM , AMERICAN CARTOONIST

What Happens if You Swallow Gum?

According to a popular saying, chewing gum stays in your stomach for seven whole years if you swallow it. Is it true? Nope! While it's true that your body can't digest natural or artificial rubber, gum will simply pass out the, ahem, other end within a few days. While it's still best not to swallow gum, there's no need to panic if it accidentally happens.

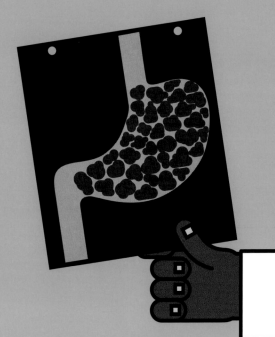

Other historic basketball players like Shaquille O'Neal and Kobe Bryant also chewed gum. Nowadays, though, NBA stars are more likely to be chomping down on something else: their mouthguards! Stephen Curry, a hugely successful player for the Golden State Warriors, often chews the clear mouthguard meant to protect his teeth from injury. Back in 2015, someone crunched the numbers and reported that Curry was more likely to make his free throws when he was chewing his mouthguard!

Football players, soccer players, and other athletes chew gum, too. Think twice before you pop a stick of gum into your mouth and lace up your sneakers, though—you don't want to swallow or choke on it!

In the United States, September 30 is National Chewing Gum Day.

CHAPTER EIGHT

POP Culture

Gum Stardom

In the mid-1900s, while gum and sports were proving themselves an all-star pair, gum companies kept looking for other matches made in heaven.

In the 1930s, Frank Fleer decided to bring bubble gum and pop culture together by introducing Fleer Funnies. These short colorful comics were included with each Fleer gum package and followed the adventures of Dub and Bub (named after—you guessed it—Fleer's very own Dubble Bubble). The gum packages also included just-for-fun fortunes, as well as fun facts and trivia.

Soon another company followed in Fleer's footsteps. In 1947, Topps launched

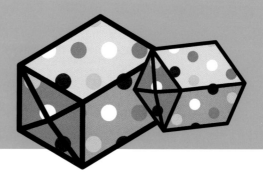

> **"Your Dubble Bubble Fortune: Your courteous behavior to older people should also be extended to those younger than yourself."**
>
> **—DUBBLE BUBBLE FORTUNE**

Bazooka Bubble Gum. Bazooka gum came with comics featuring a kid named Bazooka Joe. The gum was an immediate hit, and so were the comics, which gum-chewers of all ages enjoyed collecting.

The Golden Age of Comics

Comics have existed in some form or another for centuries. Early versions began to emerge in Japan around 1200 with scrolls featuring manga, a Japanese illustrated art form. Then, in Europe in the 1800s, it became popular to express political opinions by drawing exaggerated images of politicians, called caricatures. But it wasn't until the late 1930s when the superheroes you know today revolutionized comics in the United States. Tired by war and financial struggles, Americans of all ages loved reading about noble protectors like Spider-Man, Wonder Woman, and Superman. Modern manga began spreading across the globe starting in the 1960s, too.

Comics are still popular today, but many people call the late 1930s to 1950s the "Golden Age of Comic Books." Yes, that includes Fleer Funnies and Bazooka Joe, too!

The Doublemint campaign showed the first identical twins on television.

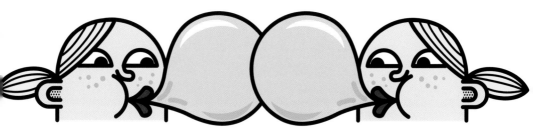

Meanwhile, gum advertising was part of everyday American life. One of the most famous ad campaigns promoted Wrigley's Doublemint. The TV campaign, which began in 1959, played on the name "Doublemint" by featuring identical twins and a catchy song. Juicy Fruit ads appealed to teens by using the slogan "Taste Is Gonna Move You" and showing different scenes of people skiing, snowboarding, and laughing. In 1975, Wrigley also introduced Big Red and targeted couples with a cheery song and romantic scenes.

Gum jingles also featured popular singers, and popular singers sampled gum jingles in *their* songs! Across the Pacific Ocean, a popular series of ads for a Japanese gum included a full love story.

The longest gum-wrapper chain stretches for 20 miles. That's more than half the width of the entire state of Rhode Island!

Gum also became a TV star in its own right. Movies started making jokes about gum commercials, and gum-chewing characters started appearing across all kinds of screens. Helga Pataki, a character from the late 1990s-era cartoon *Hey Arnold!*, built a statue of her crush entirely out of gum. In one episode of *SpongeBob SquarePants*, Patrick gave SpongeBob gum for Best Friends Day. Meanwhile, a character in *Adventure Time*, Princess Bubblegum, is literally made of gum. To this day, popular characters in TV shows continue to chew gum and blow bubbles.

Gum's star power wasn't just confined to television either. At home, children played with create-your-own-gum toy kits, and people even began to decorate their rooms by creating chains out of gum wrappers!

Rapper Missy Elliott
blows a bubble.

Celebrities got in on the action, too. Famous musicians, such as Justin Timberlake, included lyrics about gum in their music. Katy Perry and Selena Gomez were photographed blowing giant bubbles, and other musicians include gum in their music videos. In fact, even celebrities' gum pieces became famous! Wads of gum previously chewed up by famous singers and actors have sold at auctions for many thousands of dollars.

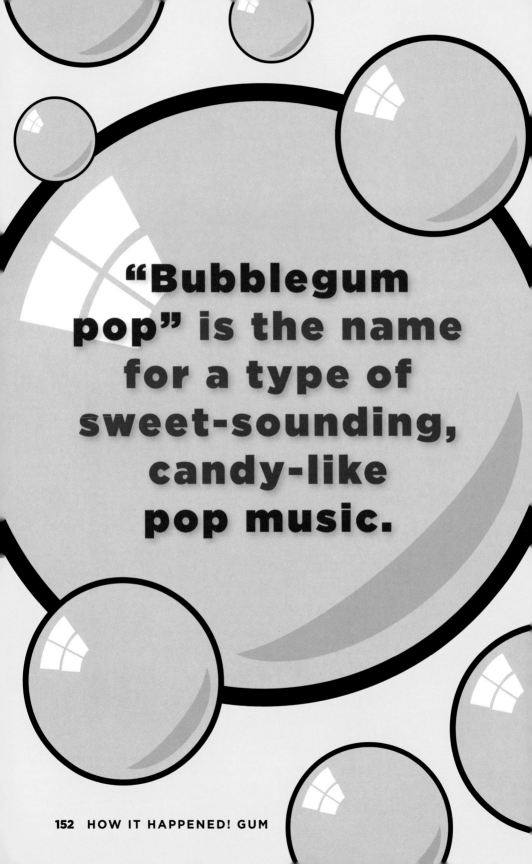

"Bubblegum pop" is the name for a type of sweet-sounding, candy-like pop music.

Insta-Pop

Want to blow the perfect bubble? Follow these steps to create a photo-worthy bubble!

1. First, pop a piece of gum into your mouth and chew until the gum is nice and soft. This activates the gum's elasticity—in other words, its stretchiness. Thanks to the way it's made, gum won't dissolve in your mouth, but it will stretch out while you chew it.

2. Once your gum is soft, use your tongue to flatten the gum against the back of your teeth. This creates a uniform surface for your bubble.

3. Keeping the edges of the gum in your mouth with your lips, stick your tongue in the center of your flat piece of gum and push it out between your lips. This helps create an extra-stretchy part you can blow into.

4. Gently blow air into the pocket you have created. The air you are blowing will push against the soft, elastic gum and cause it to expand into a bubble.

5. When you are ready, use your lips to seal the sticky ends of the gum together. This traps the air inside, giving you the perfect bubblegum bubble . . . until it pops!

The Art of Gum

On top of becoming a part of pop culture through television and movies, gum also *popped* onto the art scene . . . somewhat accidentally! In the 1990s, people lining up outside of a theater in Seattle, Washington, began sticking their used, chewed-up pieces of gum onto a wall in a nearby alley. While it started out like any other bit of litter (well, maybe a little stickier), something unexpected happened. As more and more

STRETCH

people added their own gum, it became more and more well known. Now the Gum Wall is a popular tourist destination and a work of art!

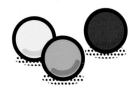

Artists have used the sticky stuff as a material to create art, too. One artist in London makes tiny "paintings" out of chewed gum. An Italian artist uses gum to carve enormous statues of bears, wolves, people—even chandeliers—and more. And once, a fan made a portrait of Taylor Swift using 17,625 gumballs.

In fact, gum has become such a huge part of global culture that it doesn't even need to be in gum form to influence things! Today, bubble gum is considered its own unique flavor and appears in everything from cakes to ice cream to popcorn. Bubblegum pink, on the other hand, continues to appear on clothing and influence designers across the globe. Does gum reign supreme?

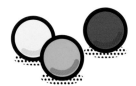

CHAPTER NINE

Here Today, Gum Tomorrow

Chewing Brings the Cha-Ching

Today, gum culture has reached enormous proportions. By 2019, the chewing gum market around the world was worth an estimated $32.6 billion—a staggering number. By comparison, that is almost three times as much as the U.S. box office (movie tickets sold in theaters around the country) made in the same year!

Asia and the Pacific Islands boast the largest number of gum sales, and the next most popular region for chewing gum is Western Europe. Devoted chewers in the United States keep the nation ranked as the third-largest gum-chewing market. Some predictions estimate that the gum industry will be worth a mind-boggling $48.7 billion by 2025.

Turkey is the country with the most gum companies in the world.

Despite these high numbers and optimistic predictions, experts have noticed that gum sales have actually been falling. In the United States in particular, sales declined more than 11 percent in the early 2010s. How could such a historical, iconic habit be on the way out? It might be due to a change in the way people shop.

Gum is usually displayed in checkout aisles, where people can easily grab a pack as they wait in line. (How many times have you suddenly wanted gum or candy while waiting in a checkout line?) In the past decade, though, online shopping and delivery made it easier for people to buy things without walking into a store. With fewer people in stores, spontaneous purchases at the checkout aisles decreased. Even those who do shop in stores tend to make fewer impulse buys these days, as

self-checkout machines let them bypass the tempting candy and gum displays.

Some countries have tried to get rid of gum completely. Singapore, a country in Southeast Asia, is famous for—among other things—being squeaky clean. How does the government do it? In part, by getting rid of gum! In 1992, Singapore banned the sale of all chewing gum in the country. They also made strict rules for what gum could enter the country through trade. Since 2004, the laws have relaxed a little, and pharmacists and dentists can now prescribe gum that is meant to be good for your teeth. But bubble gum? Forget it!

The fine for selling gum in Singapore can be as high as $100,000 U.S. dollars.

Some people can blow bubblegum bubbles with their nostrils.

Going Green with Gum

In countries besides Singapore, old chewed-up gum still litters many streets. Can anything be done about it? Yes! A company based in the United Kingdom specializes in using old gum to make new objects. The company, which collects chewed gum in containers, recycles the wads into objects including cups, rain boots, shoe soles, notebooks, and more.

"The footpaths look a lot nicer without the ugly gum marks."

—EUGENE TAN, SINGAPOREAN LAW PROFESSOR

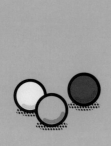

Although gum sales have been declining in recent years, the sticky stuff's reign is not over yet. It turns out that many early claims about the health benefits of gum might really be true! Studies by dentists show that sugar-free chewing gum activates the saliva in a person's mouth, which helps keep teeth free from germs. Some sugar-free gums also include xylitol (pronounced ZAI-luh-toll), a natural plant substance that can help prevent cavities.

Other scientists have found that gum's good properties might go beyond the teeth. Chewing gum might help with digestion or reduce the irritating acid that can build up in a person's stomach. And that's not all: Scientists have determined that chewing gum can indeed boost your brainpower, from making your memory better to helping you concentrate for longer.

Of course, the healthiest chewing gums are the ones with the most natural ingredients . . . which is likely why natural gum is making a comeback! Many companies are now offering gum made from all-natural ingredients and shipped in sustainable packaging. Unlike the gum of the past several decades, this gum is biodegradable, meaning it breaks down over time. Some companies are even adding natural ingredients that can supposedly help boost immune systems and reduce stress.

Other companies are taking their gum all the way back to the basics. That's right—now you can chomp on chicle or mastic just like people did centuries ago. Farmers on Chios have continued harvesting mastic—the same mastic harvested by the ancient Greeks—and touting its antibacterial benefits. In Mexico and other Central American countries, locally run organizations are sustainably harvesting sapodilla trees in ways that are safe for the chicleros.

So while gum may keep evolving—or reverting back to its original form—it looks like it's not going away any time soon. Gum is sticking around!

A Yummy, Gummy Timeline

8000 BCE

Stone Age
humans chew
on birch tar, a
natural gum.

3000 BCE

Ancient
Egyptians use
a natural gum,
gum arabic, to
help preserve
mummies.

500 BCE

People in the
Mediterranean
prize mastic
gum from Chios,
Greece, as the
best natural gum.

An ancient Egyptian mural

1300 CE

Around this time, people begin to use the word "gum."

1500 CE

Spanish invaders observe Maya and Aztec people chewing chicle, a natural gum.

1848

John Curtis
begins making
and selling a
version of the
spruce sap gum
that Indigenous
peoples in the
northeastern
United States have
been chewing for
centuries.

1869

Antonio
López de
Santa Anna
and Thomas
Adams
attempt to
turn chicle
into a cheap
version of
rubber.

1876

Thomas
Adams
forms
Adams
Sons and
Company,
one of
the first
chewing
gum
companies.

Workers in an early twentieth-century factory make and slice gum.

1884	1893	1906	1907
Thomas Adams creates Black Jack, the first gum cut into sticks.	William Wrigley Jr. creates Spearmint and Juicy Fruit.	Frank Fleer invents the first bubble gum, Blibber-Blubber, which fails.	A global financial panic causes advertising costs to fall.

1914

Wrigley introduces Doublemint.

1915

Wrigley begins an ad campaign to send free gum to everyone in the phone book.

1920s–30s

Radio becomes popular in the United States.

1928

Walter Diemer creates Dubble Bubble, the first successful bubble gum

Children clamor for gum and sweets at a confectionary in the 1950s.

1930s

The Fleer Corporation introduces Fleer Funnies with its gum.

1950s

Television becomes popular in the United States.

1952

Topps Baseball Cards are sold alongside gum.

1960s

Wrigley begins its Doublemint television ad campaign.

1975

Wrigley introduces Big Red gum and a jingle to go with it.

1980

Robert Nelson creates Big League Chew.

1988

Wrigley introduces Hubba Bubba Bubble Tape.

1992

Singapore bans the sale of chewing gum.

Today, gum comes in all different colors, flavors, and shapes.

Early 2010s

Gum sales around the world begin to decline.

2019

The world's gum industry is worth $32.6 billion.

2023

Natural gum companies are on the rise.

Chew It Yourself!

The sticky story of gum is one that involves ingenuity, perseverance, and creativity. Get your own innovation bubbling with these gum-based activities.

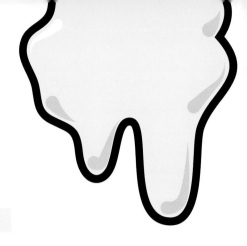

Create an Ad

William Wrigley Jr.'s success as an entrepreneur can be credited in part to his creative advertising. Pick an item, food, or place you love and create a brand-new advertisement for it. If you want, try coming up with three different kinds of ads: a print ad, a radio jingle, and a commercial.

Make It Better

Frank Fleer's first few attempts at making bubble gum were unsuccessful. Finally, his employee Walter Diemer made an improvement to Fleer's original recipe and hit upon success! What popular item do you think needs improvement? Dream up ways to make this item even better.

Invent Your Own

If you were to invent a new bubblegum flavor, what would it taste like? What color would it be? Don't forget to give your flavor a catchy name, too!

Glossary

Ancient: An earlier time in history

Chicle: The thick white sap of the sapodilla tree, found in Mexico and Central America

Chiclero: A chicle harvester

Flappers: A term describing young Western women during the 1920s who were known for taking control of their independence

Ginseng: A root often used in foods, teas, and traditional medicine

Gum arabic: A natural, light orange-pink gum made from the sap of acacia trees

Gummivore: An animal who primarily eats the gums and saps of trees

Jingle: A slogan describing a product paired with a catchy musical tune

Mastic or masticate: A soft, natural gum that can be harvested from plants and trees

Muktuk: A food consisting of whale skin and blubber

Sap: A fluid that oozes out when trees and plants are cut

Note: Some of these words may have more than one meaning. These definitions match what the words mean in this book.

Index

Image Credits

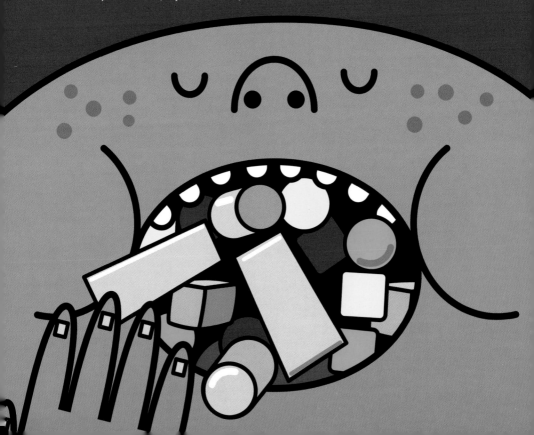